Moving ?

MOVING ?

Eldon Weisheit

EDITOR
Harold Belgum

Publishing House
St. Louis London

Concordia Publishing House, St. Louis, Missouri
Concordia Publishing House Ltd., London E. C. 1
Copyright © 1974 Concordia Publishing House
Library of Congress Catalog Card No. 73-11881
ISBN 0-570-06765-0

MANUFACTURED IN THE UNITED STATES OF AMERICA

CONTENTS

CHAPTER 1

It's Your Move

It happens every day in countless homes throughout the country. Over the telephone or at the kitchen table:

"Honey, the boss said there was this opening in Topeka." The line may be spoken with great excitement or deep anxiety — depending upon the speaker's views of Topeka.

"Why don't we go ahead and try it!" For a long time the family has talked about leaving the farm or going back to the farm — moving out West or going to the big city — starting a new business or trying a warmer (or cooler) climate.

"We're going to have to do it; so it might as well be now." The family faces special problems. Because of the health of one member all must relocate. There is a need to be nearer (or farther from) the relatives.

In each case the family is planning a move. The move will have a tremendous effect on their lives. It will determine their financial future. It can make, break, or stagnate a career. In many cases the move will influence who the future sons- and daughters-in-law of the family will be.

Huge moving vans, rented trucks and U-Haul trailers, cars loaded down and piled up, all carrying family belongings from one address to another are an everyday part of the American scene. One out of every five families moves every year — and the number is increasing. Two out of every five young families move each year.

This book is not addressed to the moving masses. It is to you—to you who are now in the process of moving your family. The fact that "everyone else is doing it" may be of little comfort to you right now. The statistics on moves do not mean that every family moves once in 5 years. Many families have never moved. Generation after generation continue to live if not in the same house at least in the same community. This may be your first move.

Or it may be that you've moved so many times you can no longer remember what your address was 2 or 5 years ago. Your children may think that people are supposed to move every year—that it's a spring ritual. You may be excited about your coming move or you may wish that for just one year you could be counted among the four who stay put instead of the one who moves.

But it's still your move.

And that's the point of this book. It's your move, and what you make of this move will influence much of your future. The move can have good or bad results—depending a lot upon your attitude about it and the way you do it. Most people agree that premarital counseling is necessary. You are fortunate if you had vocational counseling before deciding on this move, if it involves a job change. Put this book in the same category—premoving counseling.

The counsel will not deal with the technical things of packing and financing. There will be no clever little household hints about the moving process. Because many people do move each year that kind of advice is readily available. Moving companies, realtors, utility companies, even schools, are all geared to work with a moving public. They can give you the technical advice. Don't be afraid to ask them.

Instead our interest is now directed toward you as an individual and ya'll (my own moves wandered me through the Deep South for 9 years) as a family. There is really no point in packing the family china so well that not a piece is chipped on the move if your marriage or your parent-child relationships are cracked by the same move.

This book is written with the awareness that the last thing you have time to do right now is to read a book. I'll be brief and to the point. I'll even suggest a few parts for you to skip if they don't apply to you.

It's your move—to Chapter Two.

Chapter 2

Living with the Decision

The decision has been made. You are moving. Now you can start facing the realities of what it means to move a family.

We hope you are happy and excited about the move. It means a new adventure. The challenges of a different home in a new community and new working conditions may be stimulating for you. Many people enjoy moving occasionally. They feel that it gets them out of a rut and makes them younger again. From a practical point of view my wife says that moving every now and then gives her a chance to get the closets all cleaned out.

Moving can be great — or it can be a disaster or any one of many degrees between the two extremes. If you are excited and happy about your move, you may save time by skipping the rest of this chapter. But remember that it's here. Even in the best of situations, you may have doubts later. Sometimes the ideal plans don't come off exactly as scheduled and you may want to come back to this section for a few ideas on how to cope with the situation.

On the other hand, if you have the usual fears, doubts, uncertainties, or other reservations about your approaching move, now is the time to face them. Because you are busy now, and because you know the decision has been made to go ahead with the move, you may think there is no point in paying any attention to your anxieties now. But you'd better take time out for a cup of coffee and think that one over. If you have concerns about the move, they may increase the possibility that the experience will be a pain. If after the move is made you start remembering all the doubts you had about the wisdom of making such a big change, you decrease the possibility of making the move a success.

So start now and face the issues. You want to make this move. You must want to, because you're doing it. After considering all the facts of the situation, you decided to move. It is not fair, it can even be self-destructive, to later remember only part of the facts and regret the move. It is now that you are facing the move that you must consider the total situation. So take a good look at it. Be honest with yourself and agree that you want to move.

This is not some form of self-hypnosis or positive thinking by which you talk yourself into agreeing with something that you disagree with. Nor is it asking you to be a hypocrite and to smile about the whole move when actually you want to throw all the packing boxes out and lock the door when the moving man arrives.

Instead your acceptance of the move is a matter of plain, simple logic. Consider a totally unrelated, and slightly extreme illustration to see how the logic works:

You are walking down a lonely street by yourself when an armed man steps out from an alley, points his gun at you, and tells you to hand over your billfold or purse. Now it is obvious that you don't want to give that man your money. Not that you're selfish. You may buy expensive presents for others, give to your church, and be generous with anyone who asks for cash. But you don't want to give that man your money.

You don't, that is, until you consider all the circum-stances—remember the gun pointing at you. You hand over your billfold or purse *because you want to*. When you consider all of the facts, you want to give him your money. It would be foolish to take a chance of getting shot for any amount of money you could carry with you. You know that it is not the time to see if you can do what television heroes do and knock the gun from his hand.

Later on you may have some regrets—if you have no insurance to ease them. You may think of things you should have done. Possible things like carry less cash, not walk alone, and the like. More interesting things like taking judo lessons or buying a police dog or installing a burglar alarm on yourself. But none of those things were a part of the situation at the time you were robbed. Friends may give all kinds of advice about what you could have done, but when you remember the *total situation at that time,* you did the right thing. There is no point in letting regrets and "it might have been" reasoning add to the problem of the missing cash.

Now back to your move. Considering all of the facts in your situation at this time, you have decided to move. Rarely is there a situation in which all of the facts are on one side. There would be some advantages in your staying where you are. There are advantages in making the move. Adding them all up, you have decided to move. Since the decision has been made, there is no purpose in keeping a minority report on file to remind everyone of the advantages of not moving. Doing so would only help wipe out the advantages of making such a move.

Consider a couple of case histories. These are typical situations rounded off—not to avoid identifying anyone but to make them fit a more general situation. Glance through them to see if any might be similar to the move you are about to make.

CASE 1: The husband is transferred by his company to a place that he and/or his wife consider undesirable. Throw in the possible votes of a few teen-age children, and the word "undesirable" may be a little weak to describe the scene.

But it is a common event. If the family breadwinner is in the military, works for a large business operation, or is connected with any national or international organization, the orders to move will come sooner or later. More than once a business has had a banquet to honor an employee for 25 years of service. As speeches are made praising the husband, the wife recalls the 17 different addresses, the upstairs apartment where the H on the faucets was only for the sake of keeping up appearances, the house with cockroaches and earwigs, and the one time they were lucky—as they headed for the basement of a prospective home, the owner's 8-year-old son said, "I wouldn't go down there with all those snakes." The wife may smile at her memories and regard them as a part of a rich and interesting life with her man. Or she may be filled with resentment as he gets the honors.

Husband, don't wait until that banquet to discover your wife's feelings. A new job or a promotion that requires you to move to another area does not have to be accepted. As you consider the challenge and excitement of a new job, consider also the views of the family. Consider what the move will do to your personal and family life as well as to your financial and professional life. And don't just tell yourself that you are doing it for them. Explain your views and priorities so they will understand your motives for moving.

A friend of mine worked for the Post Office. He was offered a big promotion that would have required him to move to a different city. It meant giving up the house that was almost paid for, leaving married children and grand-children behind, and establishing a whole new life-style. He elected not to make the move. That decision also required him to accept all the facts and evaluate them. It required that the family understand so later they would not feel that he was a failure or resent financial limitations. They had to establish their values and live with them.

Also be fair to the boss. Don't move if you are going to blame him for all the difficulties that might come with the move. Your acceptance of a transfer is evidence of your agreement with it. Decide now if you want to continue with your present employer, and make the decision accordingly. Then live with it. Having an unseen decision-maker in the person of a distant boss can become a convenient whipping boy for all the problems of a move. But it is a bad thought pattern to develop and also limits an employee's effectiveness and future with the company.

Wife, you also have to accept certain things about your husband's transfer. You are a part of his work. Whether he tells you or not, he probably couldn't do his job nearly as well without you. You are a part of his move. Perhaps the move has already put a strain on him. Don't add to it. Be a help to him in the move rather than a liability. As you try to understand his feelings, also help him know what you think about it. If he says that he is doing it for you, be free to tell him that you have something else in mind that he can do for you—if that's the case.

You also have to consider the resentment you might cause if he regarded you as holding him back professionally. If there is a conflict on such an important decision, do not make it final on a spur-of-the-moment emotional outburst. Take time to see both sides. Talk it over in the presence of a concerned counselor such as your pastor or a mutual friend.

After all the facts are considered and a decision reached, make it unanimous. Save no room for I-told-you-so accusations when things don't go right later on. There may be many hardships that result from a move or from declining a move. During the time of problems it is easy to forget the

14

reasons why you decided to move and to think of the reasons why you should have stayed put. When that happens, it is a good idea to remind yourself that "considering all of the circumstances at that time" you wanted to move. It doesn't mean that the weather at your new home becomes any more pleasant or that you miss old friends and family any less. It does mean that you're going to live with the decision you made.

CASE 2: Same as Case 1 except the wage earner is not employed by a firm that transfers him. He is self-employed or independent enough to make his own decisions. This category includes a wide range from migrant workers to professional people. Farmers, teachers, union workers, ministers, attorneys, unskilled laborers, and numerous others find themselves in this situation. No one is going to tell them to move. They must face the decision that might uproot the whole family without having someone else to blame in case it doesn't work out. If the move sours, the family cannot unite in anger against "the big bad boss," but instead they turn against dear old dad, who already has enough problems with a bad move on his hands.

If your family has had to make its own decision about the move, you need to give special attention to living with the decision. There may have been numerous factors to consider. Another family may have been in the same circumstances and have made a different decision. But this is your decision. You are the ones who had to make it and live with it.

It might help you to consider the possible extremes—the family that moves if everything doesn't go exactly right and the family that never faces the reality that they have no future in their present situation. The first moves all the time. The second never does. Both suffer. But there are many degrees between. Consider your past record. Have you moved too often? Should you have moved sooner? Don't repeat the mistake. Talk it over with people who have decided both ways. Then remember that this is your decision.

A move will give you a new start on life only if you can do it without taking old problems along. As a general rule (meaning there are exceptions) you can't move to get away from problems. The reason is that you are a part of the move, and often we make our own problems. At the time you have an opportunity to move, you should consider ways to solve the problems first, then move without them.

CASES 3−72: There is no way to list all the case histories of why people move. Some will be mentioned and discussed in later chapters. The list could include:

> health of a member of the family.
> need to be near (or away from) relatives and in-laws.
> the spirit of adventure.
> need to be near a special school for a child.
> desire to find out what a certain part of the country is like,

and on and on the list could go. Some general ideas should be followed.

1. If the need to move is based on one member of the family (health, near to relative, special school), make sure the rest of the family understands and agrees with the need. Everyone who makes the move must see the need for the move so they do not show resentment against the one later.

2. If this is a "dream" move — to satisfy a special itch or fill a certain ambition, make sure everyone either has or at least understands the same itch and the same dream. Don't force others to share in an adventure they don't want. Don't go along in someone else's dream if you're going to ruin it.

3. Talk. Talk to each other. Talk to a counselor, pastor,

or someone who will consider your needs, not his own. And listen. Listen to each other. Listen to what others have done in similar circumstances.

Living with a decision means that you accept it as having been right in the circumstances and at the time it was made. Circumstances may change. Time does. I know one family who spent 22 years in the military dreaming about retiring and going back to their hometown, to "God's country." They finally reached their dream, went home, bought a house, and then looked around. The town hadn't changed a bit, but they had. As they learned that circumstances were different, they changed their decision and moved on. They still felt the experience was worthwhile.

Living with your decision doesn't mean that it will never be changed. This may not be your last move — so keep this book around. Make the best of this move. If everything doesn't turn out right, make the best of it. If another move should be necessary, don't waste the effort of blaming this move. Learn from it, and live with your next decision.

CHAPTER 3

Look Who's Moving with You

If you are part of a family, this is a group move. You may remember the times when you were all alone. Moving meant packing a suitcase, throwing a few things in the back of the car, and heading down the road. It's not that way anymore.

Moving a family demands the logistics skill of a general planning an invasion. The troops must be deployed. They must be fed regularly despite the fact that the can opener is packed in any one of 11 boxes marked "kitchen equipment." All of your earthly possessions must be divided into categories: (1) things to be taken in the car, (2) things to go on the van, (3) perhaps things to go into storage, and (4) in descending order, things to (a) sell, (b) give away, or (c) just leave in the house for the next occupant to worry about.

All of this together requires the educational equivalent of a master's degree in personnel management and the experience of a 20-year supply sergeant.

There is a temptation to think it would be easier if you could just do it all by yourself. A friend of mine in the military spent a year on remote assignment away from his family. He returned just in time to help move the family across country to another duty station. After 2 days of togetherness amid packing cartons and inventory sheets his wife told him, "Look, I've managed this family for a year. I'm sure I could get us moved if you'd just get out of the way."

But it is a family move. Circumstances may make it necessary for either husband or wife to take a major part of the burden alone. But if at all possible this should be a shared adventure. The act of moving requires many personal adjustments. If a husband and wife make the move together, they are making the adjustments together. All the little, sometimes insignificant decisions that must be made are more easily understood when both husband and wife face them at the same time. Neither will have to make long explanations later.

The idea of a family sharing the experience of moving might even be extended to the children. Granted it is a relief to have someone offer to take care of the children on moving day. (Remember that also when someone else with small children makes a move.) For small children it may be the only way to do it. But as children grow older, they can be involved in the move. There are several good reasons for including them. They can be of some help in doing the work. Children should learn to contribute to the work done in a family. Their sharing shows that they are part of the family. Psychologically their involvement in the move is also important As they see one house emptied, they may feel a sense of sorrow and loss. But it is a healthy feeling that must occur during such a change. Just as a funeral helps one accept the reality of death and prevents living in a dream world, being part of a move can give the children an opportunity to experience the move rather than go through the unreal act of leaving home from one address and returning home to another address.

A child's security is often shaken by a move. But the security level can be increased if he knows that his treasures are packed and will be sent to the new home. Even though his treasures may include a bottle collection, a bicycle without handlebars, and four live mice (one suspiciously plump), it is necessary to take the child's needs into consideration.

It is a truism that a family that moves together stays together, but it's worth thinking about. During a move a family is forced to consider one another's needs. Make that a good event. It is a time when the family is clearly identified as a group. In the new home there will be a time when everyone is at a low ebb. Then members of the family must depend on one another for conversation and entertainment. There has to be some good in that.

But all this good won't just automatically happen. The purpose of the move is not for family therapy. As part of the preparation for your move take a good look at the other people who will be moving with you. Consider how this move will affect them and how you can make their part of the move more pleasant.

Below is a list of possible subgroups that may be a part of your family. You can skip those sections about groups that are not part of your move. But take the time to read the section that is intended to describe you. Don't be afraid to let other members of the family know how well this description fits you and what other special needs you may have. Let them know how they can help you on this move. And listen to their evaluation of their own needs.

The Preschoolers

Perhaps the age 5-and-under group have the easiest time in any move. Yet they may get the most attention. They aren't involved in decision making and therefore not worried about being blamed if anything goes wrong. They will accept the decisions of others without argument. Their security does not depend on status (such as house, number of friends) but on love from their parents. Their emotional need for material things is limited to easily packed items such as blankets and stuffed animals or dolls. It is any wonder that Jesus said we should be like the little ones?

But there are some special considerations that should be given to the preschool gang. Some of the big dangers for them are:

1) being ignored. Moving takes a big bite out of everyone's normal ration of time. In addition to all the extra work that a move requires there is often an increase in social activity before the move and an increase in time spent shopping and on household chores on the other end. To find this extra time, parents may unintentionally take it from the children. Yet it is a time when the child needs even more parental contact, if not in quantity at least in quality.

2) being confused. When a child has just begun to learn the family routine, it is confusing to see the routine go down the drain. All the rules are suddenly changed. So the child reacts by doing a little extra yelling. The parents react by getting more tense and increasing their own audio effects. The child reacts by—. You can see how this part of the move can cause problems. The parents must break the panic cycle and give some help. It may even help the parents to get their mind back on the real things of life. Try to keep the schedule as routine as possible or understand the child's reaction when it is disrupted. Continue family customs at meal- and bedtime even though you may be in strange surroundings.

3) being deprived. Though a small child's needs are simple, they are strong. He may not need a lot, but what he needs is necessary. One of the most common words of wisdom given to parents is to allow each child to take a special toy or "security blanket" along in the car. It's good advice. But let the child make the choice. Don't take some-

thing because it will look nice when seen by relatives or motel desk clerks.

The Elementary School Crowd

One of the big concerns felt by parents is the effect a move will have on their children's education. Many families time their moves to match the school year. Often Mother stays behind for the children to finish a semester. So let's give some special attention to your children who are in the elementary school bracket.

Start with the school situation. The parents' concerns about moving the children duing the school year can be divided into two parts. One deals with the actual educational problems. The other is with the pyschological results of a move.

Educationally speaking there is no reason why children should not be able to be transferred from one school to another. Because of our nation's high mobility rate teachers and school systems are used to transferring students out and receiving new ones in during the course of the year. Some large school systems have special classes for students transferring in. The smaller systems can give more individual attention to help make the change easier.

The problem is that schools have different programs and the child may have to make some adjustments. Sometimes these differences are only that—a different way of doing the same job. On the other hand you may be moving from an inferior system to a superior one, or the other way around. Either way you have a problem.

But it is not a problem that will ruin your child's chances of going to college. It is important for the parents to know what the child has achieved in his present school, what his problem areas were, and how he integrates into the new system. If you move from a poor school system to a better one, private tutoring may be required—or at least some more help from home. But this will be needed right away. Don't wait until the gap increases. If you move from a better school to one with lower standards, you may have to provide extra challenges to keep your student(s) interested in school.

The psychological effect of the move involves the school as part of the child's total experience. The individuality of each child starts to show up during these years. Some children are very adaptable. Some are afraid of change. Know your child and be aware of what problems might be caused by the move. But don't assume there have to be problems. The kid may be glad you moved.

One advantage of moving during the school year is that the children have a ready source of new friends after the move is made. Moving as soon as school is out seems better from the other end, but it also leaves the children with a long summer in a new place with less chances to meet others their own age.

Most children in the early school years find it easy to make new friends and can easily give up old friends. We moved when our oldest son was 7. He noticed that I was sad as we drove out of the driveway, and he asked why. I told him I would miss our friends. He answered, "Don't worry, Dad. We'll make new friends." Children generally don't worry about names, occupations, or social status. They recognize other children as "their kind of people" and can make friendships.

When our second son was born, a military friend said we were fortunate to have two boys. "One boy has to go out and find friends," he said. "Two boys and a ball are found by others." He was right. If you have an only child, or one who has no acceptable sibling for playing in the yard, make a special effort to help him get acquainted. We found one faster-than-baseball way of getting acquainted. Our dog had nine pups 2 days after we moved into one community. We were an instant social success among the children. However, this method is not recommended.

The great psychological need of this age group will be continuity. Their self-identify beyond being their parents' children is just starting. Do not let the move disrupt its growth. They have developed a feeling of possession. Their treasured collections should be moved if at all possible. Make every honest effort to move all pets. If you are moving from the farm to the city, this may be impossible. But explain it. Other special problems involving pets can come up. You may have to live in an apartment (at least temporarily) that won't allow pets. If you are moving to Hawaii, there is a special problem about moving dogs. Remember the child owns the pet. Help him understand the reasons for decisions involving his possessions.

A move may also be a problem for a child because it changes the ground rules just when he was beginning to learn them. He knew what streets he could cross, where he could play, and what part of the house was off limits at certain times. Now he has to relearn the whole system.

The children should also be involved in the discussion about the move itself. This is not the time to say, "Surprise! Tomorrow we move to Greenville." Let them know about the possibility of the move. True, they cannot make the decision, but they should know that their individual concerns will be considered. Give them some choices about what they will take with them in the car and what will be packed for the van. Discuss the kind of house all would like and explain what will be possible.

On one move when our three were small they described the house they wanted: two-story, red, no grass ('cause grass ruins digging) with big places to run. We realized they were describing grandpa's barn—to them an ideal residence.

Probably no member of the family, unless it's Mother, has more to lose in a move than a teen-ager. They are finally arriving. They have their own friends. When the phone rings, odds are it's for them. Mother has finally accepted the fact that they can cross the street without getting lost. The boys have found that some girls are worthwhile after all. And girls have found that some boys have found that . . .

Then whamooooo! We're moving to Tulsa. It's a plot. A sneaky trick to pull the chick back into the nest— a different nest but obviously still parent-constructed.

Give your teen-ager special consideration. Encourage a farewell party. Provide address and autograph books in abundance. Don't try to wipe out the years you have lived at your present address with a glowing account of the future. If you have lived in your present home even a few years, it will be remembered as the place of the teen-ager's first awareness of the real important issues of life. The best friends in the world live there. The first date. The first time to drive a car happened there. Don't knock it! Your child is fortunate to have such good memories.

But you are still moving. Junior and Junior Miss are coming along. Your teen-ager may speak about going to live with a friend to finish high school. He or she is sure to have plans to spend all of summer vacation, Christmas, and perhaps Easter "back home." During a move is not the time to endorse or disapprove such plans.

Let the teen-ager be a part of the move. Let him be involved in as many decisions as possible. Show the advantages of the move for the family as a unit. Others will also have sacrifices to make. Don't bribe with promises that will pay the youngster to move with you.

Children out of the Nest

Do you have a child who has already married, is in college, in the military, or working away from home? That's one you don't have to worry about moving. But that child (pardon the expression) also deserves some consideration as you make the move.

If you lived in your present home for any length of time, that "out of the nest" child may always remember it as the last childhood home. Once you move, he no longer has a place to come home to. He can no longer go back to "my old room" or sit on the steps or climb the tree in the backyard. That person also has an emotional investment in your move.

If at all possible, get the family back together in your old home one more time. Offer the child who has moved out something from the home for his or her own room, apartment, or future home. If the child can't come back for one more visit, make the offer by mail, and send the item to him, or keep it with the understanding that it now belongs to the child.

When the grown son or daughter visits you in your new home, give them some help in feeling at home. Memories of their childhood, gifts they have made or given to you, pictures, will help them have a sense of belonging and know that they are still a part of the family.

Wife and Mother

Perhaps the greatest burden of any move falls on the lady of the house. Maybe it is stereotype thinking to see the wife as a house manager, but even in today's liberated society women feel the pressure of keeping the household in operating condition. Friend husband has his responsibilities too. Each husband and wife develop their own working relationship regarding responsibilities. They must be adjusted from time to time but, please, not during a move. Save that for the year you don't get transferred.

A move completely upsets a household routine. Storage space and working areas are different. Laundry facilities and closets are strange. As shopper for the family, the wife no longer knows which store has the best buys on meat or what day of the week is best for buying vegetables.

If one can look at the wife's job as house management (either part time or full time), it is easy to see the extra work a move makes for her. In most cases the reason for the move has nothing to do with her profession. She gets no promotion or increased status. Yet she gets the extra work. Husband and children should share in the extra work.

But the wife who is a part of your move is more than a house manager. In addition to concern about her extra work also remember her emotional involvement in the move. She is giving up a house that she did her best to make into a home. She probably has spent more time there and has done more work there than any other person in the family.

She is also better acquainted with the neighbors in most cases and may be more involved in community projects. In most cases she had to work out her own position in the community while her husband got his through his work. She's giving this up.

The wife's reason for moving is to be with her husband. Yet in increasing numbers the wife moves and then finds she is with him less than before. His new job requires more time, more travel, more attention. Suddenly the cause of all her extra work and sacrifices seems foolish. If she has to be alone, she should have stayed where she was.

In such cases the husband and wife need to be prepared for such strains before the move. Each needs to know the other's feeling. They need to be aware what demands the new job, the new house, the new neighborhood will put on them. The husband must understand that household expenses will go up as they settle in a different home. Curtains from the old house never fit the new. (But the ones from the house in Des Moines would fit. Where are they?) Different appliances are needed. There is less time to prepare food, so convenience (being translated means expensive) foods must be used. Wife, don't assume your husband will know these things unless you tell him. Or maybe I already have.

Husband and Father

The man of the house may get off the easiest in the move. In most cases the move revolves around his work. If he is transferred by his company, he may already know people in the new location. He already has a routine prepared for him.

Sometimes he needs some special consideration. The new job may not be what he expected. He must learn to work for different people or have different people work for him. He must adapt to new work regulations. At the same time he has to install towel holders and figure out why the TV doesn't work right. He recognizes (or should) that each member of the family needs his special attention after the move. But the new job also needs special attention.

The Older Folks

Just a few thoughts about the family that includes a grandma, grandpa, or other older person who has become a part of the household.

Don't let Grandma feel that she is being packed up and shipped along with the household effects. The older person probably doesn't want to move but knows there is no choice. Help them get reestablished in a routine with their own private place for a comfortable chair as soon as possible. Also remember their needs for peer-group friendships at the new place.

Perhaps there are other categories, but by now you get the picture. Recognize the stress that the move places on yourself and others. Don't think only of your problems in the move. Instead make it a family situation. Be concerned also about others and their problems. Let the others help you.

There are several things you can do together to make the move a more pleasant experience:

Use the devotions offered in Chapter 9. You may want to add more. If your family doesn't have regular family devotions, now is a good time to start. And if you already do, now is certainly not the time to stop.

Order newspapers from the place where you will soon be living. If none, or some, of your family hasn't been there before, the newspaper will make the place seem real. Make it a family project to divide the paper according to each person's interest. Mother will feel better after reading the grocery and clothing ads and knowing that stores offer good products and prices. The kids will be interested in the movies and sports events. Check for news about your church. Of course, look at the real estate ads. Notice the community events available. You'll become excited about all the new things to do and comforted by the presence of the things you are already accustomed to.

Care about the people who will move with you. Put a big label on the family: "Fragile. Handle with loving care."

CHAPTER 4

Leaving the Old Behind

There may be a number of reasons why you dread to move. First of all, it's a lot of work. But consider it a good exercise program. Most of us want to lose a few pounds or to shift some of our weight to a new location. Maybe the move will help.

Some dread to move because of the problems of settling down in a new home and community. That will be discussed in a later chapter. Others find the thought of moving upsetting because they do not want to leave their present home. This chapter is aimed at that problem. In case you are glad to move because you never could stand your present neighborhood anyway, don't skip this entire chapter. There's something at the end especially for you.

Your level of grief about leaving your present home depends on several things. For one, the length of time you've lived there. If you've been in your present house or neighborhood all of your life, this move will be a big event for you. All first experiences have some special anxieties involved, even the ones we look forward to. The first move has no previous experience to draw on. You may have heard others describe their moves. But remember people describe moves in the way they describe their operations—they give special attention to how theirs was unique. And that often means a recital of all the problems. After all, who wants to hear that everything went well? So don't be scared off by others.

On your first move you may think that handling all the details will be the big problem. However, professional movers take care of those things. If you are a do-it-yourselfer, plenty of people will offer advice. Your bigger concern may be the emotional part of the move. Going to another city or state—to a great unknown. Leaving behind lifelong friends. Being separated from relatives. When you move around, even a first cousin becomes a distant relative.

It's not just the first move that causes such problems. You will have those separation pains each time you move from a place where you have really settled down. Any area where you have had a baby born, gone through a special family crisis, become involved in community activities will have a special hold on you. It is not easy to be separated from a friend or a relative. It is not easy to give up little "security blankets" such as a tree or flower garden that you planted, a room you decorated just the way you wanted, a nice window with both a view and a breeze. To lose people or things from our life one at a time is bad enough. When you move, you give them all up at once.

First face the fact that moving causes a grief reaction that can accurately be compared to the grief reaction caused by death. The sorrow experienced at death is caused by a personal loss. I no longer have a person who previously filled a certain role in my life. This is why one can feel sorrow at the death of someone he did not know well but who was a part of a regular routine such as a gas station attendant or the security guard at work. One can even feel sorrow at the death of someone who was an aggravation in life. The aggravation may be missed.

When you move, many vacuums are created at once. Your grief will not be the most severe, because the people you love the most will be moving with you. You can also cut some of the grief by making detailed plans to return often to your former home. But after a few moves you will learn that such returns seldom happen. And when they do they can be disappointing.

There are a number of ways people express their grief at death. Most of the methods may also apply to the grief of moving. I wrote a poem about my last move. I'll share it with you:

> A short, easy lesson
> On how to say good-bye;
> Cry!

Crying is the most natural, perhaps the most helpful way of expressing grief. Thank God that our society is gradually changing so a man can cry in public without being afraid of losing his masculinity. Let's hope it does not become necessary to prove something else. Crying is helpful only if it is needed. If moving makes you feel like shedding tears, let go. Cry alone, if that's best for you. Or cry with people who will understand — members of your family or the people from whom you will be moving.

Maybe one word about crying is in order. People cry for different reasons — sometimes even because they're happy. Some also cry because they are afraid or angry. Such crying is different from crying for sorrow. Tears of grief offer a release and generally end with a wipe-your-nose-and-go-on-living attitude. A person in grief can say, "I've had my cry for today," and go on living. If you feel desperate sobs taking over and no relief from them, find someone to talk to about it. Find the cause for the tears.

Some people express grief though anger. When one is moving there are many possible targets for anger: the movers, the real estate people, the boss, and above all, members of the family. It's natural that nerves get tense and snap occasionally during a move. Talk about that ahead of time. Remind yourself and your housemates that now is the time to work together to avoid dividing up into the Red and the Blue armies.

But don't excuse outbursts of anger just because you are moving. If you are expressing grief through anger, find a better way. Because you are moving does not give you an excuse for being rude or cruel to others. If things are going wrong, recognize that your getting angry will probably increase the level of frustration rather than diminish it.

Another way people express grief is with extreme physical activity. As long as you're busy, you don't have time to feel sorry for yourself. That might come in handy when you are moving. There's plenty to keep you busy. But there are also limits to what you can do. Do not exhaust yourself physically as you prepare to move. Pace yourself. You've still got a big job ahead: getting settled in the new home. Follow good physical (and mental) health rules as you move. Good food—not every meal at a drive-in. Plenty of rest. I know this all sounds idealistic, and you'll have to bend the rules some. But at least try.

There are numerous other ways people express grief (one book lists 16), but by now you get the picture. Recognize that sorrow is natural, and be honest with yourself. Grief is nothing to be ashamed of. Think how much worse it would be if you moved from a neighborhood and didn't care. If you loved no one and no one loved you, your stay in that area must have been a problem for both you and your neighbors.

Occasionally someone suffers so much from the sorrow of moving that he decides to protect himself from such grief again. So he resolves not to become close to people in a new neighborhood. Don't care about others; then it will be easier to move.

But don't fall for that line of thinking. That's like holding your breath to avoid pollution. The cure is worse than the problem. Instead learn to understand the nature of friendships. Recognize that if you can make friends in one area, you can do it also in your new community. Friendships should not limit people. Having friends expands our view of life. It tells us that we can like people and they can like us. (See poems pp. 72-73)

It's true that you don't trade in old friends when you find new ones. You will still love the old friends too. You will keep some contact with them, at least for a while. But better yet, in this world of travel, your paths may cross every once in a while. There is always joy in meeting old friends.

Saying good-bye to places may be just as difficult. As you prepare to move, you may suddenly feel a strong attachment to parts of your neighborhood. There is the park where your son hit his first home run. Your first attempt at building a bookshelf. Marks on a wall to show how the children have grown. Each member of the family may have such memories connected with your house and community. Talk about them with each other. Take along the good memories by having pictures, clippings, souvenirs that will keep the experiences alive for you. Remember that the experience is past anyway. Your involvement in it, your achievement is a part of you. That part of you will go with you on the move.

Now that promised word for the person who is glad to get out of a community. There may be valid reasons why you are glad to move. Those that are connected with the place to which you will move are fine. But take time to consider the reasons you want to get away from your present area. You may take many of the same problems with you. If you were unhappy in your present home, find out why. And leave behind the things that made you unhappy.

There is a tendency for people to criticize their hometown. As long as it is honest self-criticism aimed at improvements, it has its purposes. But when the gripes become against people, when the attitude is "I want out

34

of here," they become a problem. All communities complain about the local drivers. Most areas have their special way of condemning the weather. There is often an element of pride in their voice as they tell how they endure such miserable heat or cold or rain. My wife and I have a standing joke that has never failed. Every time we move into a new area someone tells us the weather is unusual that season and not at all typical.

In 10 years we lived in three cities; one with about 12,000 people, one with about 200,000, and now a large metropolitan area of several million. Yet in each city the local newspaper has had a series of letters to the editor saying, "There's nothing to do in this place. The young people are all leaving." Somehow we found more than enough to do with the time and money we had available in all three places.

There can be numerous other reasons that you may want to move from your present locale: dirty politics, bad school systems, unfriendly people—you add to the list. Granted, such things may be real problems. But the same or equally annoying problems will probably exist where you will move. Every area has its advantages and disadvantages. I have often received letters from people who had been anxious to move for a specific reason but whose attitude changed after the move. They often found they only traded in old problems for new ones. At least they were used to the old ones.

It is easy to get into the habit of remembering the good things about the place you used to live, dreaming about the wonderful place where you will someday live, but seeing only the faults of your present situation. And it's a habit that can easily move with you, making you always one step behind and one step ahead of enjoying life.

Why not let this move be the one that gets you back into step? Leave behind the problems that you dislike about your present home. Don't ignore the problems of your new community, but don't dwell on them. See the good points too.

There's an overused story on the subject. Maybe it's so old you haven't heard it. So here goes:

A family drives into a small town and stops at a gas station.

"We're thinking about moving here," the man says. "What are the people like?"

"Well," says the attendant, "what were the people like where you came from?"

"Mean and no good," says the driver. "We're moving to get away from them."

"Better not move here," says the attendant. "That's the same kind of folks who live in this town."

A short time later another car drives in and the driver asks the attendant the same question. Again the attendant asks about the people in the driver's former home.

"They were fine neighbors," says the second man. "Friendly and honest. We sure hate to leave there."

"You'll like it here," says the attendant. "That's the kind of people we have in our town."

CHAPTER 5

And More Decisions to Be Made

The decision to move was only the beginning. Once you know you have to go, you must start making numerous other decisions, often in difficult circumstances. There is the rush of time, many uncertainties, and lack of knowledge about your new area. Let's consider some of the major decisions now. Maybe you've already decided on some. Maybe you've got no choice on others. If so, this will be to help you live with your decision or the one that someone else made for you. Otherwise, it is to help you consider alternatives and make the decision that is best for you and your family.

The big decision is: Where will we live? The question has two possible interpretations. One: Will we live in our own home, rent a house, apartment, mobile home, etc.? Two: What area will we live in? You don't have to live in the same town where you work. Consider both of these questions as we work through the choices you'll have.

Don't start out by looking at houses and neighborhoods. There are too many possibilities for you to look at them all. There is an urge to start looking at possible homes at your first chance. Some people must make a rapid decision because they travel to their new area to look the situation over and find a home—all on one weekend. Many a man has sunk his life's savings into a home because he thought it would make the family happy only to find that no one, including himself, likes the house and/or location.

Start out by developing a philosophy on homes. Let every member of the family be a part of the planning. Do some dreaming about what you would like to have. And be realistic on what you can afford. It is even worthwhile to write out your philosophy on a home. We did one time and sent it to a real estate salesman who had been recommended to us. He understood our message so well that we bought the first house he showed us.

Several basic questions should be asked:

Do you want to continue your present living situation, or is this the time to try something different? Suppose you now live in a house in the suburbs. To make the move with as little disruption as possible, it might be best to find a similar suburb in your new area and then find a home much like the one you are leaving behind. Most American cities, even small ones, have housing areas that are indistinguishable from one another. Their similarity can give you an instant at-home feeling. Also people who live in such areas are more likely to be in the same boat as you and as your previous neighbors. They may also be on the move. There are no deep traditions or social cliques in the area since all are new there.

The same is true regardless of where you live now—be it ghetto, farm, apartment house, or mobile-home park. You could start your search for a new home by seeking another area like the one you left. Many people do this unconsciously. It is one way to keep as much continuity as possible during a move.

But there's another side. This move could give you a chance to try something different. If you know you will be moving again in a few years, as the case often is, you might like to live in a totally different situation than before. This may be your chance to change life-styles or to see how other people live. Our last move gave us our first chance to live in a big city. My wife and I both grew up on the farm. We had lived in small towns and middle-size cities. We had been in suburbia. So we moved into the city itself. We're glad we did.

But that was our decision. You make your decision on the basis of your own family's experience and needs. Many people will try to influence you. If you happen to have friends or relatives in the area you will move to, they may try to convince you that theirs is the best neighborhood. Be complimented that they want you as neighbors, but do your own looking. Also remember that they still may be trying to prove that they made the right decision. Or they may honestly like their home, but that doesn't mean you would like one next door.

Real estate people will also try to influence you. When we told one realtor about our decision to live in the city, he totally ignored our wishes and insisted on showing us houses in the suburbs. He insisted that we'd "like it better" there. Buy or rent what *you* want, not what someone else wants to sell or lease.

There are also the social pressures of the status symbol. Don't let any possible prestige that goes with your new job go to your head. It's not true that "all the executives live in Rocky Hills Estates" or that "the most desirable people prefer Sunset Manor homes." You pay more for the status symbol. You also face the possibility that the symbol is not valid.

You must also know how much you can afford to pay either as rent or as down payment and monthly install-ments. Consider how well you were able to meet your housing expenses at your present home. Is there any reason it will be different in a new area? If you are getting a pay raise, remember that other living costs may also be higher in your new community; so you can't put all the extra money into housing.

People in real estate say that most people end up buying

or renting a home more expensive than they said they could afford. (Confession: I've done it every time.) Be honest with yourself, and know if the figure you give the realtor is maximum or minimum. If you are going to spend more than you said you could, where does it come from? A dream home can become a nightmare if you can't afford to do anything other than live in it. Check your family priorities. Are you willing to give up vacations to have a better home? Do you mind driving an older car? Decide before you sign the lease or the mortgage.

While on the subject of money, consider whether you are going to rent or buy. To rent doesn't mean you will live in an apartment. Many nice homes are available to renters. You can also buy an apartment. Condominiums give many of the advantages of apartments; yet you get the deed. A mobile home gives you a combination. You can buy the home for the investment and rent the lot. Of course you can also rent mobile homes and buy the lots.

Your length of stay at your new area should have a big influence on your decision. If you are to be there for only a short time, you might consider only renting. Some people buy homes with a sell-back clause if they plan to move again soon. Such an arrangement is often only a complicated method of renting. If you hope to be in the area for many years, it might be worthwhile to rent for 6 months or so to get well acquainted in the community before you buy a home that will be yours until the mortgage is paid off. For those between the "short-timers" and the "forevers" it is often better to buy immediately. It saves a move and gives more chance to build an equity.

Most homes are bought and sold by FHA or VA loans (that's Federal Housing Authority, available to anyone, and Veterans Authority, available to those who have been in the military). Securing such loans takes much longer than conventional loans, though many builders will let you move in before final approval. Once in awhile someone has to move back out. There is also much more red tape involved in FHA and VA loans than in a conventional loan through a bank, but real estate people have learned to live with it. Let them handle the problems. A bank loan requires a larger down payment but offers more freedom in buying and selling. A bank loan can also offer special considerations such as letting you pay your insurance and taxes direct and avoiding escrow accounts, on which you receive no interest.

Don't assume that buying a home always saves you money. You must consider the possibility of having to sell in a hurry and taking a lower price. You may lose your down payment. If your original investment is small, you are almost renting the home anyway, since most of the payment is for interest rather than principal. When you buy a home, you may have repair costs and assessments. The city or county can decide to put in sidewalks, pavements, etc., at your expense.

Under present law you can deduct the part of your monthly payment that goes for interest and taxes from your income tax. There is some talk of changing that. But as of now it is a plus for buying a home. On the other hand, remember you could be receiving interest on the money you have invested as a down payment had you rented a house.

When you are buying a home, you must consider it a financial investment. But face it, it is difficult to live in a financial investment. You may have to choose between the house that offers the best possible return on your money and one that is a better place to live. Can you afford to have a house that you would enjoy rather than one that makes money for you? It's your choice; so think about it.

Also how does your decision on a house reflect your views on social issues? Do you talk about the need for people of different races to live together to understand one another—and then buy a home in the middle of people who are of your own race? Are you willing to buy a home in an area that might change as people from a different race or nationality move in? Remember, not all ghettos are poor.

Another consideration is the "nearness to . . ." factor. Reading the "Houses for Sale" ads often makes one think that the house is surrounded by nothing but schools, shopping centers, churches, and the place where you work. Personally I prefer to be near other houses.

But you should decide where it is the most convenient for you to live. Many people spend up to 2 hours or more a day driving to and from work. Commuting takes both time and money. It is also an aggravation to many people. But there may be some advantages in living a distance from your work. You might save enough on housing expenses to pay for the extra cost of driving. A home far from work may offer more space, a chance for a garden, or something else that has special meaning to you. Then the long ride will be worth it.

Also remember that work isn't the only place to which you must drive. It might be better to drive farther to work and live near school, church, recreational centers, and the like. Then a one-car family can walk to many places while Father drives the car to work.

Another decision: new and modern vs. old and traditional. Consider family preferences. Does the modern, all-electric, amply closeted home turn you on? Or does the old, spacious, they-don't-build-them-like-that-anymore house fill you with excitement? There is no way of, and no point in, proving that one is better than the other. The question is: Which is better for your family *at this stage of life?* What was great for you 10 years ago might not be your thing now. Consider both good and bad experiences from the past, but also look to the future. Children grow up and leave home fast. They're gone before the mortgage is. Look to the future, and project what your needs will be.

Many people save money by buying an old home and remodeling it themselves. But those people also work hard on evenings, weekends, and vacations. Repairman, know thyself! Don't assume that anyone can put in a shower or wallpaper a kitchen. Moving into a new home also often requires a lot of extra work. Putting up towel racks and curtain rods is the first test of the new homeowner. Then he faces the task of landscaping. For the man who doesn't know the difference between a hammer and a screwdriver (and doesn't want to learn), the 2- or 3-year-old house is perfect. The house and yard are broken in but not broken down.

Finally, consider emotional values. The most important consideration is your own (and others' who live with you) feeling about the house and neighborhood. Such feelings may be difficult to recognize and describe, but each of us has certain values that are uniquely ours. Families should know their feelings before they start looking. We once bought a home in a city where we already lived; so we had ample time to look for the perfect home. (I know that most people don't have that time to decide on a house. Suggestion: If you haven't bought or rented recently, take the time to look at places available in your present area. Then you will have a feel for what you like and what you dislike when you start looking in your new area.) We soon discovered that my wife disliked every home without big trees in the yard. There may be no logical reason for her feeling, but it makes her feel good to drive in the driveway and see trees. I'm sure she could live in a home without trees, but why not recognize that the trees are more important to her than a walk-in closet? We've bought another home since then. It has no less than 10 big trees in the yard. I have a happy wife. Not just because of the trees but also because her values were respected.

That doesn't mean your family needs a place with trees. There is no end to the list of possible features about houses that add the touch of perfection for members of your family. To some a yard and maybe even a garden are important. To others such space is only a battlefield for crabgrass and lawnmowers. To some a fireplace is a joy — to others it's a pain in the neck and a hole in the rug. Green shutters or a picket fence are the final touch for some. An entrance hall, an open stairs, a real basement with a fruit cellar, a patio — you name it. Each family is unique and should recognize the special features of a home that appeal or repel.

Also look at a home as you will furnish it, not as it is presently furnished. Many people buy a home after having seen it with the previous owner's expensive furniture. It looks different when filled with a combination of Early Marriage and Salvation Army specials. Also see simple ways to improve the home by making it lighter or cozier. Know what you can do to make it belong to you — other than pay money. When your family puts your personalities in the house, you will feel that it is yours.

Use your imagination in selecting a neighborhood. I work in a large city and drive only 10 minutes to work. But I have co-workers who have the same office hours as I do who live in small towns, in the suburbs, and on farms. In our former home we had the opposite situation. We lived in suburbia. Friends living near us worked in small towns 50 or 60 miles away. They had reasons that made them prefer to live in the city. Maybe the interstate highways haven't added much to the beauty of America (personal view), but they have given us a chance to view more of it. People driving 50 miles to work via interstate often are on the road no longer than those who go 10 miles across town during rush hour.

After you've waded through all these ideas about a place to live, decide which features are important to you. (Be sure to include special things about you that I may have overlooked.) No one house or apartment will give you everything you want. As you start looking at specific places, you also start adjusting your requirements. One house has the perfect garage, another the perfect kitchen. The location of one is perfect, the price better on another. Then establish your priorities. Give up the least important features in order to have the most important.

Let your individuality shine through. The final decision is an emotional, not a logical one. Use logic only to narrow the field. Then walk through the house. See your family eating in it. See yourself entertaining company, celebrating Christmas. Take a walk through the neighborhood. Is this where you want to be?

We had an open house when we moved into that home that we spent 3 months looking for. One friend walked in and immediately said to my wife and me, "It's you." We beamed with joy because we felt that way too. We have lived in other places where such a remark would have been an insult. When we moved again, we were tempted to look for another house just like the one we left. But we recognized that we were changing and our environment was changing. The next house was totally different, but again it is us.

The decision about where to live will be the big one following the decision to move. But there are also others.

When do you move? Often you have no choice in the matter; so you needn't worry about it. But if you have a choice, think it over before you decide to delay the move. There may be valid reasons for delay: children finishing school, completing medical treatments, etc. But once you have decided to move, you become a family without a community until the move is made. You won't feel like doing anything in the home where you now live because you're going to leave it. You can't get involved in school, community, or church for the same reason. People who hear you are leaving tell you good-bye, tell you good-bye, tell you good-bye until you dodge them and know they may be dodging you. When you've got to go, go!

How about moving your furniture? If your company moves you, they will make the decisions and pay the bill. Lucky you. If this move is on you, you may want to consider other options. Renting a truck or trailer is practical for short moves if you have few household effects. But it takes a lot of work. A generalization is that you save half of the expense by doing it yourself. But you earn the money you save. The question is: Can you earn more at your regular work than as your own mover? Or: Do you have the money to pay someone to move you? If not, do it yourself and enjoy it.

You may have heard bad stories about moving companies. In all of our moves we have had only one unpleasant experience. The movers put our things in storage and forgot them, then made us pay for the storage. Eventually it was straightened out to our satisfaction. Looking back over many moves, I think the movers have as good a batting average as any other profession — including my own. One time a box was left behind. They discovered it and air-mailed it to us though I had assured them that we were in no rush. On one move our furniture had to go into storage (that always increases the possibility of damage — two extra handlings). Two legs were snapped off a solid oak chair. The moving company paid the bill for a highly skilled woodworker to repair it. And they didn't know that I would be writing a book about the subject.

You can also rent furniture and avoid moving heavy

items around the country. Renting furniture gives you a chance to change from Danish Modern to Early American whenever you want. Young couples or those who pay for their own moves should consider the possibility.

You will have other decisions. Should we sell the home we are now living in or keep it as rental property? Will college-age children move with us or stay behind? Add your own special problems. But don't let the weight of such decisions complicate your move more than necessary. Take the time to check things out as a family. Don't assume that you all agree on decisions until you've talked about them.

CHAPTER 6

It Will Be a Moving Experience

The move you are about to make will be a landmark in the history of your life. From it you will remember the age of children, furniture, automobiles, and clothes. You will tell your daughter she had her tonsils out before you moved to Peoria; so she had to be less than 8. After a few moves it is fun to go through the house and identify your possessions by their source. We have something from each place we have lived — not deliberately. That's just the way life is. You will know that men started wearing turtleneck shirts sometime in the late '60s because you first saw them in Dallas, and that's where you lived then.

Instead of subtracting from the continuity of life, an occasional move may add to it. Instead of seeing the years blend into decades with little to distinguish one from the other, your life is clearly divided into well-defined sections. Remember where something happened or with whom, and you can figure out when it happened.

Moving to different parts of the country also broadens your understanding of life. It is easy even in this day of modern communication and transportation to have a narrow, one-community, one-life-style view of the world. A few moves help one see that people have different customs, different values. These differences are not right or wrong issues. They are different on a horizontal plane, not a vertical one. I'm glad I've lived on a midwest farm and a Florida island, in a small southern town, two state capitals, and a large city. Each place has contributed something to my understanding of life. The combined experiences would give me the courage to try again by moving to another new situation.

All of these good things are being said about moving, not to talk you into it (you've already decided that) but to prepare you for the fact that we are now going to discuss the heartaches of moving. The big one of saying good-bye to a place you loved has already had its time at bat. Now we turn to some specialized problems that not everyone who moves will have. But they occur often enough to warrant individual attention. Some have been alluded to previously; now we give them full attention. If you're in a hurry, glance through the headings and find those that apply to you.

First Move from Home

Some will never experience this, either because they will never move or because they grew up in a moving family and never developed deep roots in one spot. But for those who have lived all their lives in one area, who know cousins down to third-twice-removed, and whose childhood friends have become adult friends, the first move is a big deal.

You are closing a chapter of your life but not the book. It is a good time to review the chapter. See how it started. Go over the cast of characters. See what events led to the end of the chapter and how they suggest the direction of a new chapter. Don't ruin the next chapter by refusing a new cast. Don't insist on living a rerun of chapter one. Life may have great new things to offer you. No matter how old you are when you make your first move, it is your chance to get a new lease on life.

A Family Divided

If you can set your own timetable to move, be grateful

and plan well. But often you can't; so adjust. Outside forces that may decide when you move include: (1) the people who are waiting to move into your present home; (2) the people who have not yet moved from the place you plan to move (because they are waiting for someone to move from another place whose occupants are waiting . . .); (3) the job responsibilities of the wage earner; (4) and a host of etc.'s, including school schedules, Sissy's mumps, and the duration of Junior's braces on his teeth. Unfortunately these outside forces don't agree with one another on a date for you to move.

The solution often is that the family moves in shifts. Like Jacob returning home in the Old Testament (he divided his family into two camps), many families must be separated during the move. Often the father has to go ahead to start work and find housing. He lives in a motel for weeks or months as he adjusts to a new job and community.

Meanwhile the wife and children contend with all the moving problems. Perhaps even the children are divided up among relatives and friends. The part of the family left behind feels left out—and stuck with chores as unglamorous as cleaning out the garage and trying to decide what must be thrown away.

But the big problem of moving a family by shifts may be that it disrupts the family relationships. Each family has established its own way of communication. Each has special little ways of showing affection and working out decisions. There are family rituals that keep members aware of one another. Most of this communication is done unconsciously because it is a natural part of life. No special effort has to be made to keep it going if it is well established. Then a forced separation disrupts everything. No longer is the family gathered around the table at least once a day to bump edges and to readjust to one another's gradual changes. Mother and Father don't share today's experiences and tomorrow's plans. They don't have the closeness of the same bed. Dad is not there to see the terrific tool chest the son found in the garbage dump or to discuss his daughter's latest views on TV commercials.

These things may sound routine, even dull to our single friends, but they are what keeps family members aware of one another. If you must be separated during the move, be aware of what you are missing. It is a time to improve communication, not to let it regress. Perhaps phone conversations will help. It's worth the cost to try. Some families enjoy letter writing—everyone enjoys letter receiving. By making efforts to keep lines of communication open you even improve the intramural social life of your family.

To a Different Climate

Moving across great climate variations presents special problems. The obvious one is wardrobe. Try moving from southern Florida to Minnesota with three school-age children. Figure the cost of new clothes for the entire family as a part of the moving expenses. Moving the other direction may sound easier, but it also will add extra cost to the clothing budget. Plus you have the problem of deciding whether or not to keep the cold-weather gear. My wife carried a pair of ice skates around Florida, Mississippi, and Alabama before moving back to a place where she could use them.

Maybe the greater problem about a move to a different climate is just that it is different. We often have mistaken views about other areas. (The reason the grass is always greener on the other side of the fence is that it rains more there.) As a native midwesterner I always thought the South would be hot and unbearable. But having lived in the South, I loved the weather. Now the thought of living in cold country (that's North Dakota to me) is frightening.

But those who have lived there say it is great—and they obviously know more about it than I do. Most of the extreme climate situations offer some special advantages. If you must live in cold areas, learn to ski, buy a snowmobile, or take up snow sculpture. If you must live in the hot zones, try skindiving and fishing and buy a hammock.

Financial Difficulties

So far we have assumed that each relocation is a move up, a promotion or a new and better job. Now let's admit that such is not always the case. There are also moves made in an effort to regroup, to try again. Some moves are necessary because a job or business has failed. Such moves are often at your own expense and at a time when your financial picture is already blurred.

So don't let the move add to the problems you already have. Special consideration must be given to such a move to make sure that it doesn't compound the problem. When the decision is made, make the move with the assurance that you are working toward a solution.

It might also help to remember past problems—those that came to a good conclusion. It is difficult to appreciate present problems, but in many cases one can look back and see how a previous difficulty led to something good. It may have helped family members reevaluate their roles. It may have encouraged someone to enter a new line of work. It may have developed a greater trust in God.

Try to find what good might come out of the present move. The good may not be financial gain. There are other important values in life. What you learn about yourself and your ability to adjust may be more important. The need to seek and the availability of outside help may add something to your life. Don't be afraid to ask someone else for counsel.

A Wife's Job Change

Because the counsel in this book must be aimed at typical situations (knowing full well that no one is typical), it has been assumed that the husband is the one who is being transferred. In most cases he is the wage earner; in all but a few he is the primary wage earner.

But it is also true that many married women are employed. Many have interesting and well-paying positions. Herein lies a special problem.

If the husband's job requires that he be transferred, the family must move. The wife must give up her job and look for another. It reduces her employment to a job rather than a career. It may make her start over and lose the value of previous work.

Or another possibility is that the wife's work requires that she be transferred. Does this mean the husband is to change jobs so she can take her promotion?

All the complications of this problem would have to be handled in a book by itself, for it involves the very concept of marriage itself. For the sake of the move priorities must be established. Whose career is considered the main source of income? Which one offers a better future, including retirement benefits? Are the careers something that help unite the marriage relationship or divide it? Special consideration must be given to this problem before you decide to move (or not to move). Solve it according to your mutual understanding of your marriage. Don't take along resentments and "look what I gave up for you" attitudes.

At the Time of Sorrow

By necessity some moves must be made at the time of great personal problems—after a death, a divorce, a major illness. Often the move is such a part of the grief that they are handled as one. In some cases this may be helpful. Moving may help you face the reality of the problem and seem like the beginning of a solution.

However, there may also be disadvantages. For example, decisions made at the time of sudden grief might not be the same as you would make at another time. Spur-of-the-moment emotional decisions often have to be remade later. If possible it might be better to delay the move until you can face the decision with more hope and better planning.

The extra work and expense of a move may add to the sorrow you already have. Again the rule "Know thyself" applies. Don't let others tell you that keeping busy is always good therapy. For some it is. For others it is another bale of straw on the camel's back.

Moving at the time of a death or divorce might also present problems about what to keep and what to throw away. It is amazing how many of your household effects are closely connected with members of the family. A move might be an opportunity to leave behind things that tend to make a shrine for a dead loved one. It is also human to be angry enough about a divorce to throw out things that you might want later. At least think about it.

On the other hand you may have anticipated the sorrow you face and prepared for what you would do. Or you may not have any choice in the matter. If the move must be made, do it and don't resent the move or you will add to your burdens. Take it as part of the cure.

The Time in Between

In any move there is a time between the day you break up housekeeping at one place and establish it at another. Sometimes that can be only overnight. Sometimes it can be weeks or months. Since our concept of home is closely connected with the place we live, it is a good idea to be aware of the strange feeling of having no place to call home.

Before one of our moves our almost-4-year-old had discovered that our house number was 222. After we watched our furniture being carried out of "222" and put in a van, we went to a motel. The son asked, "Is our number 12 now?" He had found a home in a motel! It made us wonder if we had been moving that kid too much.

But the question taught us a lesson. Everyone needs a home. Even if you spend weeks with relatives, there should be a time when you have your own family together as a group for a car ride, a walk, or just together in a room. Continue having family devotions together, or start them.

Etc , Etc , & Etc

This list could go on and on, because each family's move has some unique features that must be faced. In case your special problem has been omitted, don't think you are the only one going through such a difficulty. The fact is, there are no simple solutions to these problems. Maybe you noticed that I haven't solved the problems listed. If that were possible, we wouldn't have the problems.

But there is a principle that applies across the board. Recognize any special difficulties in your move. Discuss them with other members of the family so everyone can see each other's concerns. Don't hesitate to ask for counsel and help when you need it. Don't let problems destroy all the good parts of your move.

CHAPTER 7

New in the Neighborhoods

Yes, that's right. New in the neighborhoods! Gone are the days, at least for most of us, when one lived, worked, studied, worshiped, socialized, and played all in the same neighborhood. Most people now find themselves living in many different social structures, the geographical neighborhood sometimes being one of the least important.

It is necessary to identify the new neighborhoods to which you are moving. Rate them according to the amount of effort you intend to put into each and what you expect from each.

First the neighborhood where you live. In the old days neighbor meant the person next door. Jesus tried to expand the concept of neighbor to include people who were in need and people who filled that need—a community of people who cared about one another even though they didn't know one another. His idea has never really caught on in practice; yet let's keep it in mind as we consider the various neighborhoods.

The importance you attach to your geographical neighborhood is probably shown by the place you picked to live. As a rule apartment dwellers are not looking for strong community ties or close friends in the same buildings. There are exceptions to this generalization, but even the apartment dweller who talks about the tragic fact that no one in the unit is friendly probably does little to change the situation. Liza Minelli has a beautiful song about a girl from a New York apartment who travels around the world looking for a single man. In Europe she finds him — a tourist from the apartment next to hers back in New York. The message of the song is: "Spend more time in the hall"; but few will take it seriously.

Although suburbia is advertised as the habitat of the friendly folks, it often does not live up to its image. People can also find themselves alone in the fields of ranch houses. Everyone has good intentions, but they also have busy schedules. Air-conditioned homes keep people inside. There are fewer people sitting on the front porch as an obvious invitation for someone to drop by.

The older residential areas also may not be as open as they used to be. Crime rates have made people overly cautious. People who have lived on the same block for years already know many others and don't feel a need to get acquainted with those "new people" even though you've lived there for 2 years.

All of these pessimistic views are not to discourage you from finding friends in the area where you live. There is still a great amount of old-fashioned neighborliness going on, even in the high-rise apartments. But now people have more choice about it. You are not forced to socialize with the same people you live near. If you develop friends in the neighborhood, it will be because you like them and they like you, not just by the chance that you live on the same street.

Your new neighbors will be cautious, at least the sensitive ones, about establishing a friendly relationship until they know how you feel about the subject. To some a first-day welcome-to-the-neighborhood-we're-glad-you're-here approach seems nosy and an intrusion on your time. On the other hand, a more reserved and delayed welcome can be interpreted as cool and unfriendly. You have to find a course between the two. And the neighbors have the same right.

Within 15 minutes after we arrived bag and baggage on a hot day in one city a neighbor was there with a big pitcher filled with a cool drink. After another move we were in a house for a year when one neighbor had a coffee at which my wife met two next-door neighbors for the first time. Yet we honestly felt at home in both neighborhoods because we were treated as newcomers are normally treated in each case. We liked both areas.

Let's consider another neighborhood: the employment neighborhood. To some this does not exist outside of working hours and then only for the member of the family who works. To others the main source of friends and social activities comes from the place of employment.

It is natural that the first people one meets after a move are through work. It is also possible that you already know many people at the place of work if this was a transfer in the same company. The employment neighborhood might be the same as or at least similar to the one you left. That makes part of the move easier.

There is also a greater common bond among people who work together than among those who merely live on the same block. Co-workers share the same interests and have the same problems. They speak the same shop talk. They have something to discuss besides sports and politics, though shop talk may not rate too high on the interest scale of some. Each person makes up his own mind about how much he wants his social life to involve his business associates. A move gives you a chance to reevaluate many previous decisions.

Another new neighborhood for you will be the cultural and recreational resources of your new community. Each area has a distinctive contribution to the total spectrum of American life. The standard joke is that the natives rarely visit the attractions of their area; only the tourists and newcomers do. Go along with the gag. Be a tourist and enjoy the advantages of your new home. Others probably drive miles and spend motel money to visit the same area. Several times we planned weekend trips or routed a vacation through the city where we now live. Then it was a special treat. The same activities are still a special treat as we make use of the opportunities offered by a larger city.

Don't limit your recreational activities to the city where you live. Study the area so you know what can be done in an evening, where you might go for a day's outing, and what might be a weekend adventure. Many areas have a special weekend retreat place: the mountains, the beach, or a lake. Check the facilities and activities that such places offer. Sometimes for a small cost you can have a weekend in a setting totally different from where you live — without taking a vacation. That's the best of two worlds. Or if you live in a small town or rural area, you may have the choice of several larger cities for weekend holidays.

Give special attention to the unique opportunities in your area. If later you move from your present home and your children study about it in history or geography classes, they should have some special knowledge. But only if you give it to them. Visit your state capital. Most areas have some historical shrines. See what it's all about. Even if spectator sports or long-hair music is not your thing, go to an occasional ball game or symphony if your neighborhood offers them. You might expand your interests.

Also think of your new political neighborhood. People who move around often have a bad reputation of not voting. In the past state residence requirements defranchized many voters. But this has changed. Sometimes newcomers will not have an interest in local politics. But look at it this way: Someone held your job before you, and someone else will hold it after you move on. The same is true of your home. Political decisions affecting your home and job will not be represented at the ballot box unless you vote. You may improve conditions for those who follow you and hope the family you follow represented your new home and job when they voted.

You may have other special neighborhoods with which you want to identify. Your children may involve you in the world of Little League and Scouts. Church as a special neighborhood will be discussed in the next chapter. If you golf, paint, collect stamps, or have other hobbies, there are people in your new area who are anxious to meet you. Volunteer work at hospitals, children's centers, and the like provide other possible neighborhoods, civic clubs yet another.

By now you have the idea of the different neighborhoods to which you are moving. That you are familiar with them does not mean they will be the same as the ones you left. Not everyone will rush to welcome you with a red carpet. It's up to you to show what interest you have in each of the new neighborhoods. If you sit back and wait for everyone to involve you, you may still be sitting there when the next moving van comes. The idea that the old-timers take all the initiative in welcoming the newcomers was great in its day. But that was a day before people moved so much. The nonmovers long ago got tired of having all the parties for the nomads. And I don't blame them.

You can take the effort to get acquainted without being pushy. Don't start out by inviting the mayor over for dinner. There are other new people in the community. Share the experience of getting acquainted in a new town and get acquainted with them. Understand that people already established in any of the neighborhoods have a full schedule. In time you will be worked in. Newcomers' clubs are available in many areas. Go to a few public meetings at church, school, or some community project. You'll get acquainted.

Maybe you've heard of the Welcome Wagon. Many cities have some variation of a program that sends a pleasant lady to visit newcomers. She is a bringer of gifts and good news. But don't count on the Welcome Wagon to introduce you to your new community. In the first place, the nice lady may miss you. She probably gets new names from a utility company. If that utility is furnished by your landlord, you won't make her list. In the second place, the Welcome Wagon is a commercial enterprise. The lady's services and the gifts are paid for by the businesses that subscribe. Her call may help you find a few shopping places; this can be appreciated. She may also be a source of other information. But you'll need more.

Make an effort to get acquainted with the community where you live. If it is in a totally different part of the country than you have lived before, read up on the area, even before you move. Find out about the local heroes. Read books by local authors. Ask a librarian for books that would be required reading on the local English teacher's list.

Also take time to understand the language. Every area has its own special vocabulary. When I first moved to Mississippi, I missed several appointments because I didn't know that evening was from 1 to 5 p. m. rather than 5 to 9 p. m. I had to learn that "showing yourself" was not indecent, just bragging a little too much. Learn where "uptown" and "downtown" are.

Develop the good grace not to ridicule local customs. They may seem strange to you but obviously are not to the natives. You may not like some (I can't get used to the idea of every school, church, and club sending children out to sell a wild assortment of stuff for money-raising drives), but you are not yet in the position to change all those things. I never did get used to fireworks on Christmas Eve either — a custom at one of our former homes.

You may have your own views on such matters, but I think we will lose a lot if our country gives up those little neighborhood and regional idiosyncrasies. Every neighborhood we have lived in had a special flavor that has made us feel we have gained something by living there.

That's why it's fun to be new in the neighborhood. You are gaining an understanding of people and an area that you couldn't get as a tourist and you couldn't find in books. The varieties of experiences will give your children a much broader view of life.

CHAPTER 8

We Never Did It That Way at St. John

There is one special neighborhood left: the church. In case you're not a church member, you might think you should skip this chapter. I ask you not to, for two reasons:

First, belonging to a church and being active in your denomination where you live will be a big help in your move. That reason doesn't really turn me on, and it has little to do with my being a church member. Nevertheless, it is true. If you are a family that is on the move, your marriage and your children need the stability that active church membership offers. It is stabilizing for children to go from place to place and find the same Sunday school material, some similarity in the form of worship at church services, and the identity of church membership.

More important, for my household anyway, is that a family needs a unity in Christ. Parents cannot assume that children will inherit their faith. The church is needed as a place for all of the family to receive the Gospel of Christ. The church is needed as a place for the family to serve others as they live out their faith.

Perhaps some of the ideas suggested in this book seem idealistic. It just isn't that easy to consider other people's needs when we have problems of our own. That's where the need for Christ comes in. We can't reach those ideals. Yet we don't have to give up. Each one is forgiven for falling short. Each knows the other is also forgiven. The receiving and sharing of this forgiveness doesn't come easy. Regular worship to be assured of it and regular service to practice it are necessary.

Moving from congregation to congregation does not have to disrupt your spiritual life. In fact, it can be a blessing to you. Sometimes people identify so much with a certain congregation or pastor that they forget the real meaning of their faith. When that happens, religion becomes a cultural or social endeavor rather than a living relationship with God and people. Moving makes you aware that your faith is in something more than the comfortableness of being a part of the traditions of a congregation.

A 30-year-old couple became active in a congregation where I was the pastor. It was the first time they had gotten involved in a congregation and found the spiritual joy of knowing Christ. When they were transferred to California, they were concerned that they would lose this new joy. I told them that it might be best for their faith for them to learn that it was not in our congregation. A month after they moved our church received a letter from them. It started, "Hey, you are right. Christ lives in California too."

As you make your move, you should be as concerned about your spiritual life as you are about the finances of the family and the education of your children. Consider the following situations, and see if they fit you.

You're going to be in the new area for only a short time. How often people use that as a reason for not attending church when they arrive in a new community! But it's not logical. You take the time to get a place to live and the utilities hooked up. You get the children into school. Why not also go to church the first Sunday you arrive in your new community?

Also transfer your church membership to your new area if you are going to be there for any length of time. Each denomination has its own way of accounting for membership changes; so I won't go into the details. In case you don't know how to transfer your family's membership, call (or write to) your present church office. Tell the congregation that you are moving, what your new address will be, and ask how to transfer.

Of course you can always be a guest in a church. Some people have been visitors of a congregation for years without joining. And they are welcome. But when you become a member, you are saying that you want that congregation to feel a responsibility toward you and you feel a responsibility toward them. It is not only a matter of financial support (they'll accept checks from nonmembers). It's like being on a team. Being a member says they can count on you. At least it should.

Don't keep your membership "back home" for sentimental reasons. The congregation to which you belong has a responsibility for you as long as you are on their records. It is difficult for them to minister to you if you live far away. If there are reasons you can't transfer (and sometimes there are), don't forget that you still belong to the church back where. Keep them posted on your latest address. Tell them your faith is still alive and well. Tell them your spiritual needs.

What if you move to an area that has no church of your denomination? First, what do you mean by area? There may not be a church on your block or even in your city, but there may be one within driving distance. I know people who have driven 50 miles one way to church regularly. They thought it was worthwhile. You'll have to evaluate that yourself.

Next your denomination has some kind of mission board. Ask them for help. There may be other members of your denomination in the area, and plans may be under way to start a congregation. Or you can be the start. Or your denomination may provide lessons and taped services for you by mail.

What if you find a church of your denomination but it seems different from the one back home? It happens every Sunday. But consider what the differences are. Are they spiritual differences? Or are they only differences in forms of worship and methods of administration. Often people find fault with small changes. Then you have to ask yourself what your faith is all about. Are you interested only in keeping certain traditions? Or are you interested in spiritual food? Check the New Testament use of the word "traditions." Five times out of six traditions are described as harming rather than helping our spiritual life.

Then there's the feeling that the church is unfriendly. It doesn't bother us if people at ball games and movies don't speak to us, because everyone goes as an individual. But churches are to be the body of Christ. Members are to care about one another. Therefore we can feel strange and left out after being in a new church. But take time for a second look.

For one thing, maybe the people next to you were also new and wondered why you didn't welcome them. That happens often in places where many people are on the move and in tourist areas. Maybe someone else didn't welcome you because they thought you were an old-time member who showed up for worship services for the first time since last Easter. Others may have been busy or just self-centered. It happens—even to Christians.

Take the time to sign the guest book or card. And write—make that print—so the name and address can be read. Also use your new address. Some people forget and use their Silver Spring address in Seattle.

Then there's the problem of getting acquainted with

a new minister. A woman once told me, "I feel at home now. My doctor and my minister both know my first name." Her point was that if you need either for help it is difficult to talk to a stranger. But don't be afraid. The faith you share with a minister will help you get acquainted.

Better yet, get acquainted before you need the help. One family, who moved often, had a baby shortly after they came to our congregation. I called on them, arranged for the baptism, and got to know them well. When they left a few months later, they said they had felt more at home in that congregation than others and closer to me as a pastor. I explained that the new baby had given us a chance to get well acquainted as soon as they arrived. I suggested that they have a baby each place they go or, as an alternate plan, invite the pastor over for dinner or a cup of coffee after they move to a new place and frankly tell him they want to get acquainted. They said they would try the second suggestion.

If you happen to become a member of a church that is dull and content with the status quo, you have some decisions to make. Don't let it destroy your faith. You can go to another congregation. Or you can stay and add some new life to the less exciting church. Think about your concept of a church member. Do you react only to how things affect you? Do you say, "We didn't do it that way back at St. John's"? Church membership involves giving as well as receiving, understanding as well as being understood.

Above all, don't let this move be a move away from God. Being human, you'll find excuses to slack off on church activities. Being saved by Christ, you also have reasons to live a full life of worship and service to Him.

CHAPTER 9

Devotions for the Move

The Last Devotion at the Old Home
Read Ruth 1:15-19a

The story of Naomi and her daughter-in-law Ruth is often used for weddings. Actually it's about a family, or all that was left of a family, as they prepared to move. Naomi had lived in the land of Moab for a long time; Ruth had lived there all of her life. Now Naomi decided to move back to the place of her birth. Ruth decided to go along.

The Bible reading is about the two women as they prepared to move just as our family is now preparing to move. They faced some of the same problems and had to make some of the same decisions as we have.

Notice that they went as a family. Ruth didn't have to go along. Her husband, Naomi's son, was dead. But Ruth wanted to stay with her mother-in-law. We also will move as a family. We belong together. We both need and want each other. We are leaving behind many friends, but we have each other.

Ruth was willing to live where Naomi lived. Their home was not a certain house in a certain country. It was where they were together. We have called this place our home. Soon we will be at a different address, but it will be the same home. Because it is our home. It is where we are together.

Ruth had learned to know God through Naomi. She wanted to remain with her mother-in-law's God. We have God with us. Christ has promised to be with us wherever we gather in His name. He has been a part of our lives here. He will be a part of our lives there. We will have to get used to new neighbors, new friends, new teachers. But we will have the same Savior. He will continue to love us, to forgive us, and to keep us close to Him.

Prayer Suggestions: Thank God for the blessings you have received at your present home. Ask for His protection on your move. Pray for family unity and a special ability to understand one another's feelings during the move.

While on the Road
Read Genesis 28:10-19

The Bible story tells about Jacob when he was in a situation like ours. He had left the home where he had lived. He was on the way to a new home. He was alone, but we have each other. He had done wrong and had to move. We are moving because we want to. There are other differences, but there are also similarities in our moves.

Jacob was going to a new place. He did not know people there. He would be facing new experiences. He felt alone. We are like that. But Jacob was not afraid, because God spoke to him and promised a blessing for him. God also speaks to us. He has sent His Son Jesus to be our Savior. Through Jesus God has called us back to be in His family. We have Jesus as a part of our family.

God has given us a special blessing. It is the blessing of His presence. We are going to a new place, but He is there. He was with us where we used to live, He is with us on the road, He will be with us in our new home.

Let's hear one of the special blessings Christ speaks to us: "Abide [that means live] in Me, and I in you. As the branch cannot bear fruit by itself unless it abides in the vine, neither can you unless you abide in Me. I am the Vine, you are the branches. He who abides in Me, and I in him, he it is that bears much fruit, for apart from Me you can do nothing." (John 15:4-5)

Prayer Suggestions: Pray for the friends and loved ones where you used to live. Ask for God's protection on the remainder of your trip. Discuss special family needs that should be included in the prayer.

In Your New Home
Read Luke 2:1-7

Did it seem strange to read the Christmas story today? The story is not only about the birth of God's Son on earth. It is also about a family that moved. When they arrived in their new city, they had no place to live; so they stayed in a barn. Joseph soon found a house for his family. The Bible tells us that when the Wise Men came, the family of Jesus was in a house.

We are in our new home. We can think about the problems we had on our move. They are nothing when compared with those of Joseph and Mary. But the point is that Jesus come into a family like ours — one that was new in the neighborhood. They had to get settled down, as we have to. They had to move again later on, as many families today do.

We can be glad that God became a human being in Jesus. As the God-man, Jesus became a part of our life. He had pain and joy, hunger and contentment, work and pleasure, death and resurrection. He also moved as we have. In one sense He moved again recently because He moved with us. He is a part of our home.

In our prayers we will dedicate our living in this house to God. We pray:

Lord Jesus, we thank You for being the One to welcome us to our new home. Please remain not as a guest but as

70

a member of the family. Be with us as meals are prepared and with us around the table as we eat. Live with us in our living room. Guard us as we sleep in our bedrooms. Furnish our home with Your love, forgiveness, and understanding by filling each of us with love, forgiveness, and understanding.

This prayer is a beginning of our worship of You in this house, O Lord. You'll hear from us again and again, and we also want to hear from You again and again. Amen.

Lord, You're Holding Out on Me

You gave me love, Lord,
   unlimited,
      unrestricted, usable love.
And You told me to love.

At first I was afraid,
   afraid to love
      and afraid to be loved.
But Your gentle prying opened the door.
I was loved!
And I loved!

But yesterday one of those whom I love,
   and who loves me,
Came to say good-by.

Another came today for the same reason.
   Two farewells in twenty-four hours
      is too much, Lord.
   And it was Your love that
      caused the ache.
When You said good-by to Your friends,
   You added:
      "And remember!
      I will be with you always."
But I could only say:
      "In heaven there will be no farewells."

You have given us love to share, Lord,
   and we shared it.
We believe Your promise of an eternity together.

Why have You kept all the omnipresence
   for Yourself?

I'm Not as Smart as I Thought I Was

Couldn't You let me know that I am wrong
    in a more gentle way?
You didn't have to hit me over the heart
    to make me see Your answer.
Or did You?

I felt so noble about saying good-by
    to my friends.
I knew Your love caused the pain.
And I knew You knew it.
I really thought You unfair not to share
    Your omnipresence with me
    so I could continue to love
    and be loved by my friends.

Then everywhere I went I saw Your love
    and Your presence.
I do not love just two people.
    I love people.
I am not loved by just two people.
    I am loved by people.
My friends are loved by
    others who have received Your love.
They love others by
    the same love with which they love me.

By Your being with each
    "two or three who are gathered together
    in Your name,"
You bring me to be with the same two or three,
    and they are with me.

I am not alone.
My friends are not alone.

Addresses